The Work Is All

Mark Vinz

The Work Is All

A Gathering of Poems

Red Dragonfly Press
Minnesota, 2011

ISBN 978-1-890193-35-5

Library of Congress Control Number: 2011922738

Acknowledgments are printed at the back of this book

Typeset in Quadraat and Quadraat Sans
    a digital type design by Fred Smeijers

Printed in Minnesota by BookMobile, Inc.
    a wind-powered company

Published by Red Dragonfly Press
    Press-in-residence at the Anderson Center
    P. O. Box 406
    Red Wing, MN 55044

To order additional copies or other titles visit:
    www.reddragonflypress.org

Contents

Author's Note

During most poets' working lives, writing about poetry or poets becomes a kind of occupational hazard. Such writing usually pays homage to certain individuals and their work, or celebrates a friendship, or elegizes a loss—and sometimes all three. I've been especially fortunate to have known many wonderful writers, although sometimes only through their poems. Sadly enough, many of the pieces in this collection have been written after—and sometimes occasioned by—the deaths of some of these individuals, but also in the sure knowledge that we all live on as long as our words are remembered.

It is to these writers that this collection is dedicated.

The Muse

It's a place I've been in before—
three calendars, all wrong,
two fans to lap the waves of smoke
from one wall to the next,
an old formica counter top
with red and black amoebic swirls
and crusted egg to bump the plates against.

Menu? she says. Her name is Melody.
You look like hot beef and fries to me.
Ashes from her Lucky Strike
tumble toward my coffee cup.

You know, I've heard all the lines
at least twice, she tells the fry cook
spread out like a stain in the corner booth.
Business has been slow.

So what'll it be? she turns and asks.
Hot beef and fries sounds fine.
Trust me, she says, and
slops the coffee to the rim and past.
I hardly ever lie.

Sleepless, Reading Machado

I

Beneath the desklamp
these small songs,
a sea wind bearing
tiny yellow flowers,
a sleeper moaning
in another room.

II

Consider for this moment
the joy of solitude,
the grief of empty rooms.

So little changes:
not the ship, or the storm,
or the eternal hunger of
the waves. Only the faces,
the fear of going down.

III

And this:
new snow in the night
covering the fresh
spring grass. Bird
tracks wandering alone
in the moonlight.

Some call it sorrow,
some call it love.

IV

Toward morning
the words grow darker
against the page.
Darker and longer
beside the clock radio
humming to itself on a table,
and the wind
just moving the curtains.

Someone whistles
beneath the window,
and footsteps walk away—
my own song returning
as the first light
gathers in the trees.

Occupational Hazards

> "I'm a poet. Catastrophe is actually
> good for my work." – Andrei Codrescu

Perhaps you've heard how we set out each morning
to scan the skies for tornado clouds, the woods for
careless sparks, the streets for ruptured mains.
We've divorced all our spouses—a few good lines
squeezed out of each—estranged our parents and
children alike. What bastards we are, they say,
and we can't deny they're right. Maybe if we wrote
stories, there'd be some way out of it, some god
from the machine chiseling escape tunnels
beneath tsunami waves or percolating lava.
The really hard part, of course, is never knowing
where it will be coming from—whatever falls from
the skies—forever hoping it will flatten thousands.

Ars Poetica

At $12.95 we just can't afford it,
my students say of the book of poems
I've recommended.
It's not even 100 pages, you know.
For that kind of money they could buy—
no, I don't want to hear
what they could buy.

It must be hard to make a living
writing poems—that much they understand.
But do you get paid by the line or page?
Fat poets with slim volumes, I joke—
a line from Dylan Thomas I've carried for years.
Is he related to Bob Dylan? they ask,
wide-eyed with connections.

Today we speak of what we can and can't
afford, this business of making a living
wringing words from who knows where,
of paying by the line or page or more.
Today we speak of craft, connections
lost and gained, and how, like everything else,
the price is always going up.

Distances

"Writing...is like driving a car at night.
You can see only as far as your headlights,
but you can make the whole trip that way."
— E.L. Doctorow

No, I haven't been writing much lately.
You need a change of scenery, my friend
tells me, and the first thing I think of is
my grandmother dying, years and miles away,
and how each time I'd drive to visit her
there'd be something to write down, some
little thing I hadn't thought about in ages—
shaken loose by highways, headlights,
an old woman sure each visit would be the last.
Even now, in the callow light of morning
I can't help wondering why getting there
always seems to take such a long time.
It's the coming back, isn't it—
so much quicker than we've imagined,
but filled with words at every dark turning:
You know you'll never see the likes of me again.

The Trouble with Poems

Say that you are reading this poem
and something you don't want to happen
does. You remember your father
chasing you down the street with his belt.
What was it you did?
Can you remember, or were there
too many times to remember?
That's the trouble with poems.
You never really know just
where they're going to take you—
like this late afternoon light
and outside the window
fir trees laden with cones
bowing like dancers in the wind.
That's better, isn't it?
Then what about that wind,
the storm coming, the trees
disappearing into waves of snow
and you stuck somewhere miles from home
in a snowdrift, with no more than
a few minutes of gas left in the tank
that you should have filled yesterday,
but you forgot, and now you might die
alone way out here because you're stupid,
because you don't know how you'll
ever explain this to your father,
who is out searching for you.
Poems are like that, you say,
and he just looks at you and shakes
his head. If I had my belt with me,
he says, I'd teach you about poems.
And you know that he already has.

Two Poetry Readings

University of Kansas, mid-1960's

I. AN EVENING WITH THE MASTER

The name, of course, still fired my memory,
or maybe I went just because it was free,
surprised, at any rate, to find the
college auditorium half empty
for Basil Rathbone, in the fading flesh,
sharing poetic treasures from the past,
the man who'd amazed us as Sherlock Holmes
in all those classic films—on stage, alone,
with an easy chair from someone's office,
small table, lamp, and oriental rug,
a kind of dingy living room to match
his well-worn double-breasted movie tux.
An hour and a half he paced and posed—
what they used to call an elocutionist—
belting out the oldies, from Poe's raven
to Keats' urn, until that famous voice
began to fray, and all the footlights dimmed,
back across those years of dreadful horror flicks
and cameos, while he stood there, hands clasped,
smiling gauntly in shades of black and white—
one of those living legends we could tell
our friends we saw one night, and nevermore.

2. The Homecoming

A lot of students went to the reading,
perhaps because we'd heard of Langston Hughes—
a man close to tears that afternoon, for
being praised and welcomed back to Kansas.
And then he read us poems about the days
when civil rights weren't yet a movement,
holding us with the painful grace of what
we knew was right, all of us, even the
full professor who'd dozed through most of it
then asked about a theory for those short
poetic lines our speaker pioneered.
Hughes just smiled at him and shook his head,
then told us when he started publishing
his poems and found they paid him by the line,
he'd chopped every one in half to make each
poem longer. The full professor snorted
and the rest of us roared, carried away
by something unforgettable—those words,
even then, we knew we'd keep coming back to.

After Reading *Morning Poems*

For Robert Bly

A long time ago you told me
I was far too fond of easy choices
in my poems—words like *darkness*
and too many others to remember now,
except that I probably hated you
for saying that, the way I hated
my father for always being right.

Now that *darkness* is drawing closer
than I could ever have imagined,
there are fewer and fewer words I trust—
only the ones like *fond*, which I used
a few lines back, and *gift*, and *thanks*.

Nightfishing

You're out at night with a small seine,
trying to find something worth keeping.
You throw out the net and haul it back
empty, torn open, filled with the usual
garbage. Nothing surprises you anymore
but the next cast, or the next—
you'll work all night if you have to,
knowing it's probably stupid, it's
probably not the best way to spend your time.
Your wife is getting anxious, the children
wonder what's happened to their old man,
moody as dark river water.
But you don't do this very often,
you tell yourself—it's a trip you've
put off too long to stop now. And then
there's a small flash of something
tangled hopelessly in the netting.
You can tell it's not what you wanted,
but you keep on working. If there's one,
there will have to be others.

After a few nights of this
you might have something worth keeping
after all—the results of your casting
spread out before you on a table.
Here, you say to your wife, take a look
at this and tell me what you think.
It's good, she says, squinting in

the room's flat light—but then, I
don't know much about nightfishing.
Look at this, you say to your friends,
the ones who know something about nets
and rivers. Unusual but interesting,
one says; another talks of trying
different, stronger nets, like his.

Sometime later, when you're finally at a
stopping place—work's not finished,
just abandoned, as some wise nightfisher
has said—you decide to send out word
of your catch, knowing that no one will
probably notice, not really, anyway.
No matter, the river's high again tonight,
swollen with run-off from a rainy season.
You feel the old tug of the moon,
the net's quicksilver flash into dark water,
disappearing, beyond all promise of return.

Lines

for Joe

Out in the boat last night we watched still air
suddenly filling with mayflies—as far
as we could see or move they came in waves.
Today their delicate remains are lined
on cabin screens, and once again the air
is thick with wings, this time from dragonflies,
dark and deliberate in their searching.

A single day, the mayflies come and go,
and now we see their helpless tracks laid down
on top of water where fish keep rising.
Only by chance we notice how these lives
complete themselves—another set of lines
to read and ponder for their grace alone,
another quickly disappearing page.

Lessons

"Writing is hard and writers need help."
– Richard Hugo

Strange how it all comes back from time to time,
the night you read here more than 30 years ago
and called to ask if I could drive you to
the place you'd read the next night, 80 miles
away. Who could have known that we'd be stopped
by blowing snow or that we'd have to wait
beside the interstate till it let up,
the only storm that never worried me
for I had hours of stories, talk of poems—
the streets you walked in failing mining towns,
the times your life broke down, and Italy,
the field of wind you wrote about the day
that you got lost in '44, a young airman
who was taking notes he never dreamed would
one day bring him fame—and then, that other
young man listening, who never would forget
the way you said all art is failure, though
our poems mean that we somehow have a chance,
the way that sudden storms can change our lives,
remind us just what does and doesn't count.

Work in Progress

Paris

A lovely day for strolling down the Champs
beside a dozen quaint sidewalk cafés
where writers, mostly in berets, are busy
with their notebooks, a glass of wine, pernod—
you can't help feel you've entered more than one
novel, story, poem, perhaps to linger there—
tall man with gray beard, curious, looking like
he has no better place to go. Beyond,
near every monument, the beggars wait—
mostly girls, who hand you soiled pages
speaking of fear for their unborn babies,
the need to get back home, wherever
home might be imagined. All around you
as you walk, words on paper, theirs and yours—
so many different languages and yet
in every one a story that you know.

Housman's Grave

"And I will friend you, if I may
In the dark and cloudy day."

The roads are narrow through the Shropshire hills,
where Sunday bells have ceased their faithful toll.
Gray skies seem fitting here, deserted towns,
and then the shrine at Ludlow, carved in stone
at St. Laurence's church. Beneath the name
and dates, someone has laid a laurel wreath
atop a garland of spring's briefest white—
for you, who pondered fame and loss so well,
who taught us heart and craft of elegy.
The valley darkens as we drive away
to meet road signs with names we somehow know,
toward other hills—our own, other turnings
unpredictable, but taking with us
the fire of flowering branches on the slopes.

The Last Time

for James L. White

I can't stop thinking of the last time I saw you—
how you looked so tired and so severe,
how I just wanted to hug you
and say it's all right, to lie a little
just to make us laugh again.
And I'd tell you, if I could,
that the last time should be different—
heat lightning on a warm night
and us just sitting on a front porch swing
to watch the families coming home
from the drive-in movie.
And we'd talk for hours in soft voices
till the rain started coming down near dawn.
Then you'd go in to shut the windows
and fix us a snack
and I'd light the last cigarette,
the one we'd been saving.
And we'd think of everything we shouldn't do
all over again, and maybe then
I could get to that place
where the weeping finally starts.
No, I don't know what it means to die.
It must be quite beautiful, you say.

At the Funeral of the Poets

for Alec Bond

It would be an old house, I think,
somewhere past the edge of town—
40 good acres of oak and pine,
a little river with a boat for fishing
and deer to come and drink in waning light.
There would have to be birds
so we could learn the names and sounds again,
perhaps a pasture with a horse or two,
rooms with books and photographs
and crocks of homemade beer.

When the screen door creaks you'll know
they're going to call us in to eat—
roasted corn and ribs, three kinds of bread
thick sliced and warm, and soup so
rich you'll wonder where you've never lived
to taste such soup as this—and the wine,
and all night long to sit in front porch swings
or stroll around the yard, listening
to each voice from the shadows—
quick small breezes bearing scents of
flowers and far-off ripening fields, and lights
in upstairs rooms that burn into the dawn.

The Last Time

for Tom McGrath

Your room, the nurse tells me,
is the one with the scanner in it—
that, and not to be afraid to wake you.
Most patients here sleep too much anyway.

You seem to know me at first,
when you ask for a beer and cigarette,
but then all light fades and you
shudder beneath blankets, clutching
at the tubes that grow from your arm.

What are you doing here? you say.
We'll miss the dance tonight.
And how about those fences that
need mending? Have to keep them out,
you know—all of them trying to get in.

What can I do? I keep asking,
beside the small red numbers forming
on the screen above your bed.
Old friend, we've finally reached the place
each road leads somewhere else.

I'll be gone for awhile, you say—
but you keep on watching as I
bend toward you, closer and closer,
farther and farther away.

Passing Through

> "We all know our names here."
> – James Welch

I've heard it called the High Line, Highway 2
still arrow straight through Blackfeet land, the
broken towns that hope leaked out from years ago.
It's what you wrote about, a paradox
a voice that sang so sweetly came from here
and learned to master registers of gray,
as if November were the only month.

I've come that way just once, your poems forever
in my ears—a guide to far corners, as you
called them, rivers always high enough for
drowning, and dirt, the place where all dreams end.

Montana is an endless state of mind,
what travel books still designate The West—
wild or mild or sold to some new wave of
outside interests every day. Just so, the past
is legend here, repeated like the lines
some drunken cowboy croons in what
is taken for the last good bar around.

For those who care to read, there might be other
lines to learn, lines we know we'll never have
the right to sing but still a necessary guide
for endless drives, and ways to mourn the dead.

One Day

> "Time was we / thought we had time on our side."
> — Raymond Carver

He was a lot younger than I am now
when he died, but already famous.
All those poems and stories about how
he'd failed, and then the rising from the
ghost-ridden ashes.

        I met him after
a reading, where we talked about his
getting back here for a visit in the fall.
His postcard came that summer. Too sick to
do any traveling right now. But who knows?
Maybe one day.

        All poems are love poems,
he said, and this one too, which I send out
like another postcard. Life has been good,
though as you knew, we still give ourselves to
all the wrong things. As for the fishing, well,
it can only get better. Wish you were here.

Points of View

"How seldom we see anything...we haven't
willed ourselves to see." – Paul Gruchow

Perhaps it was the book of poems I read
before I fell asleep, perhaps another
night of restless dreams that left me lost.
I wake this morning with some new resolve
to notice what I usually miss—
outside the window, how the early light
has etched my neighbors' chimneys into spires,
the reckless chirp of one small bird that rises
over all the others in the crowded hedge,
a little girl in a yellow dress who's found
a piece of 2x4 and throws it down and
jumps and picks it up and jumps again,
a kind of hopscotch without squares or friends.
There's nobody else on the sidewalk today,
but at the corner, waves of vehicles
roll by, full of throbbing bass notes, full of
faces stuck to cell phones, staring straight ahead.

A Man of Words

for Jay Meek

I can't help but think of you tonight as traveler,
in your old white-linen suit
strolling out into the piazza
notebook in hand, jotting down each detail,
each scent and sound to assemble later—
back in your room at the shabby little hotel
or on the deck at midnight crossing.

Against the cool damp air you've bought a hat,
which you keep taking off and putting on again
as if you'll never quite get used to it,
or maybe it's the idea of wearing hats.
You'll have to think about it,
about crossings and stars—all those stars.
If there's one thing you've depended on
it's old friends. You jot down a few lines
in your notebook, though it's too dark to see clearly,
and try the hat again—which seems
for a moment to fit just right—and stroll out
on the deck among the stars, listening hard
to those engines throbbing beneath you,
and somewhere in that rush of steel and wave
the tiny pulse of something else that leads you,
growing louder in the night air.

Landscape with Hawk

> "No longer do we darkly lie alone."
> – John R. Milton

Prairie sun breaks through the clouds
and shifting light across the grass
confounds the eye again: this is
the place we must be taught to see.

A searching hawk soars upward now,
soon lost within immensity,
above the fading wagon ruts,
the hidden arrowheads and bone.

As quickening wind brings thunderheads
the lone hawk soars—a sentinel
for all the land-bound words that seek
to track its solitary way.

Still Life with Crows & Poet

for Bill Elliott

Not long before an old friend's sudden death,
crows began appearing in his poems.
Be careful it doesn't happen to you,
another writer warned—as if that omen
might simply be forgotten, shooed away,
or I could fail to hear their raucous numbers
gathering in trees outside my windows.
Some summers they wake me every morning,
though now, in January's listless cold,
bare branches seldom seem to hold them.
Only an occasional straggler today,
as much a colleague as a hoarse intrusion,
searching for some shiny thing to break the spell,
some piece of news to get excited about,
to remind everyone who still has ears
of all that gets taken for granted.

For Friends Who Send Poems

In with the blare of circulars,
tidy notices in anonymous envelopes,
lurid promises of fortunes to be won,
there is a small package with my name on it,
light seeping from tears in the wrapping.
For a moment, everything stops:
I turn a book of poems over in my hands,
fingering the sheen of the cover,
the curve of each letter.
I see a face beside a window, expectant,
looking up with the thinnest smile,
and at that moment I remember
just how unfaithful I am:
I will abandon each page that
calls me to one of my own;
it may take years before I finish reading.
Then I see another face by the window,
my face, and I know again
that what we give, we get back,
what we lose, someone else will find for us,
and what is sent out will stay
beyond all finishing and forgetting.

Absences

The message that's recorded on the phone
is unmistakably bad news, and then
another call tells us it's one we love—
a sudden death while traveling, somehow
appropriate for one who always
seized life too completely to stand still.

A door slams shut, a wall has dropped away,
and once again I'm driven back to
empty pages, insufficient words,
to rooms he always filled on entering—
rooms lined with books, piano music, and
good friends who raise their glasses one last time.

And now, as all the lights are blinking off
in every prairie town we've ever loved,
when all the toasts are made and songs are sung,
when leaving is the only certainty,
a single voice keeps echoing, along
each dark, untraveled hallway of the heart.

The Work Is All

> "Any day's writing may be the last."
> – Roland Flint

It's taken the death of an old friend, a poet,
to drive me back to these notebook pages
I'd abandoned, to puzzle out in words
what my heart seems so dumb to.
But words are the places we've lived,
he and I—if not wisely or greatly,
then with amazement and even, sometimes,
that grace we didn't know we'd been given.

"The work is all," he said in a poem,
knowing too well how little will get read—
but also the need to send a prayer each day
for all those good words that manage to come,
especially now, as the waning winter light
dapples notebook sheets and books of poems alike,
that place where old friends smile and weep together.

Acknowledgements

"Ars Poetica," "Occupational Hazards," "Two Poetry Readings," "After Reading Morning Poems," "Lessons," "Passing Through," "One Day," "Points of View," "Landscape with Hawk," "Still Life with Crow and Poet," "Absences," and "The Work Is All" are previously uncollected.

"Sleepless, Reading Machado" is from *Climbing the Stairs* by Mark Vinz, 1983

"The Muse," "At the Funeral of the Poets," "The Last Time, for James L. White," The Trouble with Poems," and "For Friends Who Send Poems" are from *Mixed Blessings* by Mark Vinz, 1989.

"Nightfishing" is from *Minnesota Gothic* by Mark Vinz, 1992.

"Distances," "The last Time, for Tom McGrath," and "A Man of Words" are from *Affinities* by Mark Vinz, 1998.

"Lines," "Work in Progress" and "Housman's Grave" are from *Long Distance* by Mark Vinz, 2005

"The Last Time," (for Tom McGrath) first appeared as a broadside, published by the Rourke Art Museum, Moorhead, Minnesota.

Grateful acknowledgement is made to the following periodicals for poems which originally appeared in them, sometimes in slightly different form: *Abraxas, Hayden's Ferry Review, Mankato Poetry Review, Minnesota Monthly, North Dakota Quarterly, Passages North, South Dakota Review, Thunderbird,* and *Zone 3.*

"The Work Is All" first appeared in *The Hudson Review*.